The purpose of this study guide is to provide supplemental educational material. It is not intended as a substitute or replacement of ROMEO AND JULIET.

Published by SuperSummary, www.supersummary.com

ISBN – 9798645399665

For more information or to learn about our complete library of study guides, please visit http://www.supersummary.com

Please submit any comments, corrections, or questions to:
http://www.supersummary.com/support/

TABLE OF CONTENTS

Romeo and Juliet is one of William Shakespeare's best-known plays. First performed before 1597 (the date of its earliest known printing), it has been popular and influential ever since.

This summary refers to the 2011 Folger Shakespeare Library edition. Your edition's line numbers may vary slightly.

Plot Summary

A feud between two noble families, the Montagues and the Capulets, is tearing apart the city of Verona. Young men allied with these households fight each other in the streets. At last, the violence gets so bad that the city's Prince declares that any member of these clans caught fighting will be exiled from the city.

Meanwhile, Romeo, the romantic young son of the Montagues, is suffering: He's lovelorn over a girl named Rosaline, who doesn't return his affections. His friends Benvolio and Mercutio persuade him to crash a masked ball thrown by the Capulets, in the hopes that he'll spot another girl to fall in love with there. This plan works all too well: The disguised Romeo falls instantly in love with Juliet, the Capulets' daughter. This is inconvenient, to say the least. Not only are the lovers' parents locked in a feud, Juliet is considering a marriage proposal from the eligible young Count Paris. However, Romeo and Juliet's love overwhelms all such considerations, and when Romeo comes in secret to Juliet's garden in the night, they vow to marry.

Romeo's friends take a dim view of this plan. Benvolio points out that Romeo was desperately in love with another girl five minutes ago; Mercutio will only make sex jokes; and Friar Lawrence, Romeo's priestly friend and mentor, warns him that "these violent delights have violent ends" (2.6.9). However, Friar Lawrence also sees the young lovers as an opportunity to heal the rift between Montagues and Capulets, and agrees to marry Romeo and Juliet in secret.

Before any good can come of this clandestine marriage, tragedy strikes when the rash and flamboyant Mercutio gets into a street fight with Juliet's cousin, Tybalt. Mercutio is killed, and a grief-stricken Romeo murders Tybalt in revenge. Though it means leaving behind his new bride, Romeo must flee Verona to avoid punishment at the hands of the Prince.

Juliet is horrified when she learns that her new husband has killed her cousin, and even more horrified when she learns that the "choice" her parents offered her about whether to marry Count Paris was not so much a choice. She bravely decides to stand by Romeo and goes to Friar Lawrence for help. He concocts an elaborate plan to reunite the newlyweds: He'll give Juliet a drug that makes her seem as if she's dead, when in fact she'll just be in a brief, deathlike coma. While her family entombs her, Friar Lawrence will send a message to Romeo to come and find her.

Juliet goes through with this plan, but Friar Lawrence's part in the proceedings doesn't go so well. News of Juliet's "death" reaches Romeo in Mantua before Friar Lawrence's explanatory message makes it there. Romeo rushes to Verona, where he finds and kills the mourning Paris outside the Capulet tomb. He descends into the dark and, finding what seems to be Juliet's corpse, poisons himself.

3

Friar Lawrence arrives at the tomb to care for Juliet as she awakes, only to find her discovering Romeo's still-warm body lying next to her. The priest tries to convince Juliet to come away, but she refuses, and he flees at the sound of approaching footsteps. Left alone, Juliet stabs herself with Romeo's dagger. In the wake of these horrors, the Montagues and Capulets, having lost the hope of their future heirs, are forced to make a tragic peace.

Acts I-II

Prologue Summary

A narrator, known as the Chorus, appears and lays out the whole story for us. Two families from the Italian city of Verona, the Montagues and the Capulets, are fighting out an "ancient grudge" (1.Prologue.3). The children of these families will fall in love and die, ending the grudge between their families. It's now the job of this play to fill in the whole story.

Act I, Scene 1 Summary

The play proper begins with two boastful young men, Gregory and Sampson, exchanging a series of increasingly filthy puns. They're from the house of Capulet, and they're swaggering around the streets looking for trouble from the Montagues. They find it; a fight breaks out in the street. One Montague, a young man called Benvolio, tries to break up the fight, but Tybalt, the ferocious nephew of Lord Capulet, won't allow this, and attacks him. The heads of the families, Lord and Lady Montague and Lord and Lady Capulet, come upon the scene. The old Lords want to get in on the fighting, but their wives hold them back.

The brawl at last breaks up when Verona's ruler, the Prince, arrives. He tells the Montagues and the Capulets that he's sick of their nonsense, and that he'll execute the next Montague or Capulet caught fighting in his streets. He orders Lord Montague and Lord Capulet to come speak with him, and the crowd sheepishly disperses.

Lady Montague asks Benvolio if he's seen her son Romeo, who doesn't seem to have been present at the fight. Benvolio tells her that Romeo has been moping in the woods around the city. The Montagues aren't surprised, as Romeo has been doing this a lot lately. None of them understands why.

Romeo appears, and Benvolio questions him. The miserable Romeo says that his moping is because he's "Out of her favor where I am in love": He's pining after the lovely Rosaline, who wants nothing to do with him, and who has in fact made a vow of chastity (1.1.173). Romeo reflects on the paradoxes of love: "A madness most discreet,/A choking gall, and a preserving sweet" (1.1.200-1). Benvolio suggests that the best cure is to go and look at other pretty girls until Romeo is distracted. Romeo says that this will never work, for the lesser beauty of others will only remind him of Rosaline's supreme beauty. Benvolio assures him that it will work, and he'll prove it.

Act I, Scene 2 Summary

Lord Capulet and the young Count Paris are discussing the Prince's edict. The chastened Capulet thinks he and Montague should be able to keep some kind of peace. Paris has other things on his mind: He wants to marry Capulet's young daughter, Juliet. Capulet is reluctant: Juliet is only 13, and his last living child. Her young age doesn't dissuade Paris, who comments, "Younger than she are happy mothers made" (1.2.12). Capulet evasively suggests that Paris should come to the feast he's throwing tonight, and look at the other girls, in case he likes one of them better.

He sends a servant out with invitations, but the servant can't read, and asks Romeo and Benvolio for help. It turns out that Rosaline is invited, and Benvolio sees in this fortuitous party a perfect opportunity to distract Romeo: "Compare her face with some that I shall show,/And I will make thee think thy swan a crow" (1.3.93-94). Romeo, still melodramatically absorbed in his own misery, agrees to go so he can pine after Rosaline in person.

Act I, Scene 3 Summary

Lady Capulet has come to her daughter Juliet's room to deliver big news. Juliet's old Nurse is there, too, and the two older women go through some comical wrangling to establish Juliet's age (only 13). The garrulous and filthy-minded Nurse has many fond memories of Juliet as a baby. She delights in retelling an anecdote about her (now-deceased) husband making a joke at toddler Juliet's expense, the gist of which is that falling down face-first is what little girls do, while young women fall backwards for sexual dalliances:

> 'Yea,' quoth he, 'Dost thou fall upon thy face?
> Thou wilt fall backward when thou has more wit,
> Wilt thou not, Jule?' And, by my holdam,
> The pretty wretch left crying and said 'Ay' (1.3.45-48).

Lady Capulet is not as amused by this as the Nurse is. She's come to ask Juliet if Juliet feels ready to be married. Juliet is taken aback: "It is an honor that I dream not of" (1.3.71). Lady Capulet notes that she herself was married at around Juliet's age and sings Paris's praises (with the Nurse's leering help), comparing him to a beautiful book that needs only a beautiful cover to complete it. Juliet agrees to look at Paris at the feast tonight, and obediently agrees to try to like Paris: "I'll look to like, if looking liking move./But no more deep will I endart mine eye/Than your consent gives strength to make it fly" (1.3.103-5). The

Nurse is overjoyed at the prospect of her darling's marriage.

Act I, Scene 4 Summary

Romeo and his Montague friends are making their way to the Capulets' party. They've picked up their buddy Mercutio on the way—not a Montague or a Capulet, and so officially invited where the others are not. Regardless, they're all going in disguise. Mercutio, a charismatic, flamboyant, and mischievous young man, is giving Romeo a hard time for his persistent moping, making dirty jokes at his expense: "If love be rough with you," he counsels, "be rough with love./Prick love for pricking, and you beat love down" (1.4.27-28).

Romeo replies that he had an ominous dream this evening. Mercutio launches into an elaborate and sinister monologue on his own dreams of Queen Mab, ruler of the fairies, as she travels by night distributing visions and making mischief. (See the "Important Quotes" section below for the full text of this speech.) Romeo interrupts this reverie; Mercutio snaps out of it, saying that fantasy and dream come and go as quickly as the wind (1.4.102). Romeo reflects to himself on his dream—a foreboding vision of "some vile forfeit of untimely death" that will be set on course tonight (1.4.118).

Act I, Scene 5 Summary

Lord Capulet, in an expansive mood, is greeting his guests. He welcomes the masked Montagues, not recognizing them, and reminisces about his own youthful days of masking and dancing. Tybalt recognizes Romeo, and tries to rat him out to Lord Capulet. Lord Capulet holds Tybalt back. Romeo is behaving himself well, and has a good reputation; Lord Capulet won't have him come to harm in his house. Tybalt persists, and Lord Capulet scolds him for overstepping. The sulking Tybalt stands down, but vows that this isn't over. Meanwhile, Romeo sees Juliet and falls instantly in love with her: "O, she doth teach the torches to burn bright! [...] Did my heart love till now? Forswear it, sight,/For I ne'er saw true beauty till this night" (1.5.51-60).

He approaches her to ask for a kiss. Their first meeting takes the form of a sonnet as they trade lines: Romeo presents himself as a pilgrim to Juliet's holy shrine, and Juliet points out that pilgrims use their lips for praying, not kissing. (See the "Important Quotes" section below for their exchange.) At last, Juliet agrees to kiss him, and the two only have eyes for each other until Juliet's Nurse interrupts to tell Juliet her mother wants a word with her. While Juliet obeys, Romeo asks the Nurse who Juliet is, and learns the terrible news that she's Lord Capulet's only child. Juliet goes through the same process, but rather more subtly: She asks her Nurse the name of several different gentlemen, only ending with Romeo. She has also fallen in love, and despairs: "My only love sprung from my only hate!" (1.5.152).

Act II, Scene 1 Summary

The Chorus appears again to recapitulate the action so far, and to tell us about the difficulties the young lovers find themselves in: In spite of their desperate passion, there's nowhere safe for them to meet. However, the Chorus observes, "passion lends them power" (2.1.13), so they'll figure it out.

Benvolio and Mercutio are out in the street looking for Romeo. Mercutio tries to conjure him up with a "spell" that's mostly dirty jokes about Rosaline:

> The ape is dead, and I must conjure him.—
> I conjure thee by Rosaline's bright eyes,
> By her high forehead, and her scarlet lip,
> By her fine foot, straight leg, and quivering thigh,
> And the demesnes that there adjacent lie,
> That in thy likeness thou appear to us (2.1.19-25).

Benvolio observes that this is only going to make Romeo mad, and Mercutio replies with more dirty jokes. At last, they give up, and retire to bed.

Act II, Scene 2 Summary

Romeo, hiding in the Capulets' garden, has heard all of his friend's sexual innuendo, and scoffs, "He jests at scars that never felt a wound" (2.2.1). Soon, Juliet appears on her balcony. Hidden below, Romeo looks up at her with longing and awe: "But soft, what light through yonder window breaks?/It is the East, and Juliet is the sun" (2.2.2-3). (For the full text of this famous speech, see the "Important Quotes" section.)

As he watches, Juliet begins to speak—and, to Romeo's joy, she's speaking about him. Musing to herself, she wishes that Romeo might "Deny thy father and refuse thy name,/Or, if thou wilt not, be but sworn my love,/And I'll no longer be a Capulet" (2.2.36-39). Names, she goes on, are just words: Roses would still smell sweet if we called them by a different word. If Romeo could just give up his family name, she'd be all his.

At this, Romeo leaps out of the shrubbery and swears his love to her. Juliet is understandably startled, but is also delighted. She starts asking practical questions, such as, how'd you get over the wall into this garden? Romeo can give only rapturous poetic answers.

Juliet goes on: She knows she should hold back and deny what he's overheard her say, but she just can't. She's aware that her eagerness may seem overly forward by the rules of the time, but vows she'll be a truer lover than women who play games. She asks Romeo to swear love to her as she has to him, but when he tries to swear by the moon, she stops him: The moon is too changeable to swear on. Instead, she tells him to swear on himself—and then stops him altogether. This is all too sudden, "Too like the lightning, which doth cease to be/Ere one can say 'it lightens'" (2.2.126-27).

The Nurse calls Juliet to come inside. As Juliet stalls her Nurse and speaks to Romeo, her worries about the speed of their attachment melt away. By the end of the conversation, she has made Romeo vow to send word to her tomorrow if he wants to marry her. The two have a hard time parting; they can't stand to be out of each other's sight. At last, Romeo leaves the garden, promising to send Juliet word of his intentions the next day.

Act II, Scene 3 Summary

Friar Lawrence, a monk, is collecting herbs in his garden at daybreak. He muses on the qualities of nature: There's nothing in the world that doesn't have some good purpose. Poisonous plants can have good applications—but healthful plants, misused, can become poisonous: "Virtue itself turns vice, being misapplied,/And vice sometime by action dignified" (2.3.21-22).

An elated Romeo breaks in on these musings. He and Friar Lawrence have an affectionate, familial relationship. Noting that Romeo seems to have been up all night, Friar Lawrence worries that he's been with Rosaline. His pleasure in learning that Romeo has forgotten her quickly dampens when he hears that Romeo is in love with a new girl and wants Friar Lawrence to marry them right away. Friar Lawrence scolds his young charge: "And art thou changed? Pronounce this sentence then:/Women may fall when there's no strength in men" (2.3.84-85). In spite of his weariness with Romeo's flakiness, Friar Lawrence agrees to perform the marriage, as an opportunity to heal the rift between the Montagues and Capulets.

Act II, Scene 4 Summary

Mercutio and Benvolio are again wondering where on earth Romeo has gone. They've heard that Tybalt sent Romeo a challenge, and Mercutio compares Tybalt's skill in fighting to that of the folkloric Tybalt, an archetypal cat in a series of popular stories about Reynard, the prince of foxes. Romeo appears, and Mercutio mocks him for his love and gives him a hard time for ditching them last night. The two exchange one of their customary series of sex puns. This cheers Mercutio up: "Why, is this not better than groaning for love? Now art thou sociable, now art thou Romeo, now art thou what thou art, by art as well as by nature" (2.4.90-93).

The Nurse appears with her servant Peter in tow. The young men all mock her pomposity and her malaprops until she reveals that she's here to speak to Romeo. Romeo chases the other boys off and apologizes to the Nurse for their rudeness. The Nurse, somewhat mollified, tells Romeo that she's come from Juliet—and warns him that he'd better not be playing with her heart. Romeo's assurance quickly wins her over. Romeo tells the Nurse to ask Juliet to come meet him at Friar Lawrence's monastic cell that afternoon to be married. He also asks her to be ready to receive a rope ladder he's made; this will give him access to Juliet's room that night. The joyful Nurse begins reminiscing about Juliet's childhood again, but at last departs to give Juliet the good news.

Act II, Scene 5 Summary

Juliet, meanwhile, is waiting impatiently at home for the Nurse to return. Love should be able to communicate as quickly as it acts, she thinks: "Love's heralds should be thoughts,/Which ten times faster glides than the sun's beams" (2.5.4-5). If only the Nurse were young like her and remembered what this felt like, she'd be jogging home. The Nurse turns up, and spends a comically longwinded time getting herself settled and comfortable before delivering any news to the increasingly frustrated Juliet. At last, she tells Juliet that Romeo will meet her at Friar Lawrence's cell this afternoon.

Act II, Scene 6 Summary

At Friar Lawrence's cell, Romeo is champing at the bit to be married. Friar Lawrence tries to counsel him to be moderate:

> The sweetest honey
> Is loathsome in his own deliciousness
> And in the taste confounds the appetite.
> Therefore love moderately. Long love doth so.
> Too swift arrives as tardy as too slow (2.6.11-15).

Juliet arrives, and Friar Lawrence can see that neither of the young lovers has any intention of taking his advice on temperance. Regardless, he leads them away to their marriage ceremony.

Acts I-II Analysis

The densely woven and often funny language of Acts I and II creates a vivid world. The Verona of *Romeo and Juliet* is a hotbed of sex, passion, and fantasy. As we discover in the very first scene, no word can be trusted to hold only one meaning, and usually those meanings lead us straight down the path to a sexual play on words. Whatever might be on the surface, the people of Verona are quick to link it to sex.

The young lover Romeo is perfectly adapted to this world. A boy of intense but changeable passions, he can transfer his undying love from Rosaline to Juliet as quickly as Mercutio can make any innocent turn of phrase into a sex joke. Both language and experience are slippery in this world.

This slipperiness sits uneasily next to the inarguable force of the passion that conquers the young lovers. While Romeo's buddies (and, through them, the viewer) have some cause to smile at the swiftness with which Romeo falls for Juliet, the play doesn't mock the real strength of their feelings for each other: They're caught up in an intense and fantastical love that makes them see each other as cosmic figures, gods, and the sun and stars. This emotion is also deep and real. That *Romeo and Juliet* is famous as a play about true love (and not about two teenagers who get in over their heads) speaks to Shakespeare's evocation of the world-conquering force of infatuation.

Many of the play's characters look on the power of emotion and imagination with a jaded and even a fearful eye. Among these, Mercutio stands out. Seemingly lighthearted, he is quick to give in to fear at the immateriality of emotion and the changeability of the human heart. His Queen Mab speech, is at first whimsical, but gets darker and darker as he engages with the sometimes-sinister power of fantasy.

In this shifting and paradoxical landscape, Juliet is the most grounded character. In the balcony scene, she muses on the malleability of names as compared to the permanence of a thing's real identity: "That which we call a rose/By any other name would smell as sweet" (2.2.45-46). To Juliet, some things are simply true—though she'll have cause to eat those words when she later bewails the real-world power of the word "banished."

Act III

Act III, Scene 1 Summary

Mercutio and Benvolio are wandering the streets of Verona. Benvolio is trying to persuade Mercutio to get out of the sun; it's a hot day, and the Capulets are roaming around. However, Mercutio is in a punchy mood, and teases the peaceful Benvolio, calling him a hothead.

They're interrupted when the Capulets arrive. Mercutio, still in a temper, starts verbally sparring with Tybalt, trying to provoke him. Tybalt doesn't want to fight Mercutio; instead, he's after Romeo, and when Romeo arrives, Tybalt challenges him to a fight. Newlywed Romeo has no interest in fighting his wife's cousin, and tries to make peace. However, this only enrages Tybalt—and Mercutio, too, who sees Romeo's refusal to fight as capitulation.

Mercutio calls out Tybalt: "Tybalt, you ratcatcher, will you walk?" (3.1.76). The two fight. Benvolio and Romeo try to separate them, and in the confusion, Tybalt mortally wounds Mercutio. In a final virtuosic and punning performance, Mercutio speaks of his injuries and dies cursing the houses of Capulet and Montague alike:

> No, 'tis not so deep as a well, nor so wide as a church door, but 'tis enough. 'Twill serve. Ask for me tomorrow, and you will find me a grave man. I am peppered, I warrant, for this world. A plague o' both your houses! (3.1.100-4).

Enraged and grief-stricken, Romeo pursues Tybalt and kills him. Now under a sentence of death from the Prince, and having killed his wife's cousin, Romeo cries, "O, I am Fortune's fool!" (3.1.142). Benvolio urges him to run away. When the Prince and the Capulets turn up, Benvolio explains to them what has happened. The Prince declares that Romeo is exiled; if Romeo ever shows his face in Verona again, he'll be killed.

Act III, Scene 2 Summary

Juliet, unaware of all that has happened, is waiting impatiently at home for Romeo to come and celebrate their wedding night. In a rich and vivid speech, she begs the sun to hurry up and set:

> Lovers can see to do their amorous rites
> By their own beauties, or, if love be blind,
> It best agrees with night [...]
> Come, gentle night; come, loving black-browed night,
> Give me my Romeo, and when I shall die,
> Take him and cut him out in little stars,
> And he will make the face of heaven so fine
> That all the world will be in love with night
> And pay no worship to the garish sun (3.2.8-27).

The Nurse arrives, wailing, and delivers the terrible news: Romeo has killed Tybalt. Juliet is distraught. At first, she curses Romeo's name, but as soon as the Nurse speaks ill of him, she reverses course: "Shall I speak ill of him that is my husband?" (3.2.106). She loses herself in grief, less over Tybalt's death than over Romeo's banishment. Her earlier thoughts about the significance of words recur, as she bewails the power of that one word, "banished." She vows to take to her bed and die. The Nurse says she'll go find Romeo and bring him to comfort her.

Act III, Scene 3 Summary

Romeo is with Friar Lawrence, bewailing his fate. He, like Juliet, turns the word "banished" over and over, seeing it as the worst possible thing that could happen to him: "O Friar, the damned use that word in hell" (3.3.50). Friar Lawrence counsels him to be patient: If he's not dead, there's hope.

The Nurse appears to fetch Romeo. She tells them that Juliet is in much the same state as Romeo, wailing and weeping. Romeo draws his dagger to stab himself, but Friar Lawrence exasperatedly holds him back and points out all the good luck that's come their way. Juliet is alive, Romeo is alive and not under sentence of death—they'll see each other again. He tells Romeo to go to Juliet, and then to flee to Mantua in the morning. Romeo, relieved, agrees.

Act III, Scene 4 Summary

Lord and Lady Capulet speak to Paris of their family's misfortune, and agree to hurry forward Juliet's wedding to him. It's Monday now; they'll celebrate the marriage on Thursday morning. Paris speaks of his eagerness, and Capulet sends him away. Lady Capulet readies to tell Juliet to prepare for her wedding.

Act III, Scene 5 Summary

The next morning, Romeo and Juliet wake up in bed together. They're reluctant to let each other go, and trade words about whether the birds they're hearing are nightingales (birds of the night, which mean they can be together), or larks (birds of the morning, which mean they have to part). At first, Romeo insists that they're larks, and Juliet nightingales—but then Juliet remembers that Romeo is under the threat of death, and changes her mind: "Some say the lark makes sweet division./This doth not so, for she divideth us" (3.5.29-30).

The Nurse comes in and hurries Romeo away. Romeo climbs out the window, and the lovers make a slow, tortured farewell. Juliet has a foreboding vision: "Methinks I see thee, now thou art so low,/As one dead in the bottom of a tomb" (3.5.55-56). At last, Romeo departs for Mantua.

Lady Capulet appears at this inauspicious moment and tells Juliet that she's going to be married to Paris on Thursday. Juliet, outraged, declares that she won't do it: "Now by Saint Peter's Church, and Peter too,/He shall not make me there a joyful bride!" (3.5.121-22). Lord Capulet appears, and flies into a rage at Juliet's disobedience, having apparently forgotten his earlier idea that she should have some say in her marriage. He says he'll disown her if she doesn't agree to marry Paris. The weeping Juliet turns to her mother for comfort, but Lady Capulet offers none.

At last, Juliet falls into the arms of the Nurse. The Nurse advises her to be reasonable: Romeo's banished, so she should marry Paris. After all, he's very handsome. Horrified by this betrayal from her surrogate mother, Juliet withdraws and runs to Friar Lawrence.

Act III Analysis

Act III changes the whole tenor of the play. Though Acts I and II set us up to expect the worst, the actual events of the story were technically a comedy—a story that ends in marriage. The deaths of Mercutio and Tybalt transform this plot into a tragedy.

Mercutio in particular plays an important part in setting off the chain of events that leads to the story's terrible ending. Mercutio's death comes as a shock to the audience: Until now, he's been a figure of comic relief, an elegant clown who's there to puncture the absurdities of his lovelorn friend. This was not the kind of character you'd expect, by conventional standards, to be killed—and certainly not in the middle of the play. The shocking loss of Mercutio makes death real. If even a word-bender so alive to the ridiculousness of humanity is mortal, then no one is safe.

The events of Act III unravel steadily from this point, often returning to the unreliability that Mercutio was always so quick to point out. One by one, the adults around Romeo and Juliet prove that they are just as temperamental, passionate, and changeable as their children—often more so. Juliet remains loyal to Romeo even after he kills her cousin; however, even the uncomplicatedly loving Nurse proves herself a betrayer.

Act III is the fulcrum of the play, and it makes clear the real stakes of human passions: Even feelings as shifting and changeable as the wind have real consequences in the world.

Acts IV-V

Act IV, Scene 1 Summary

Friar Lawrence is speaking to Paris, who thinks that Lord
Capulet wants him to marry Juliet quickly to stop her
mourning Tybalt. Friar Lawrence considers what to do
when Juliet appears. She puts Paris off, telling him that
she's here to make her confession to Friar Lawrence, and
Paris withdraws.

The despairing Juliet asks Friar Lawrence to provide her
with some alternative to suicide; she's ready to stab herself
if the marriage to Paris can't be prevented. Friar Lawrence
comes up with an idea: If Juliet has the strength of will to
kill herself, she might also have the strength of will to go
through with a dangerous plan. Juliet eagerly agrees:

> O, bid me leap, rather than marry Paris,
> From off the battlements of any tower,
> Or walk in thievish ways, or bid me lurk
> Where serpents are. Chain me with roaring bears,
> Or hide me nightly in a charnel house,
> O'ercovered quite with dead men's rattling bones,
> With reeky shanks and yellow chapless skulls.
> Or bid me go into a new-made grave
> And hide me with a dead man in his shroud (4.1.78-86).

Indeed, this is something like the plan. Friar Lawrence
explains: Juliet will go home, agree to the marriage, and
then take a drug he'll provide. This drug will induce a
death-like coma. Believing Juliet to be dead, her family
will bury her in the family tomb. Meanwhile, Friar
Lawrence will send a messenger to Mantua, calling Romeo
to come and rescue his bride. Juliet will awake in the tomb,
Romeo will be there to collect her, and the two can run

away to Mantua together. Juliet eagerly agrees, grasping for the drug: "Give me, give me! O, tell me not of fear!" (4.1.123).

Act IV, Scene 2 Summary

Juliet returns to her father, and tells him that in her discussion with Friar Lawrence she has seen the error of her ways. She agrees to marry Paris. Her father is delighted: "My heart is wondrous light/Since this same wayward girl is so reclaimed" (4.2.48-49).

Act IV, Scene 3 Summary

Juliet absently looks over wedding clothes with the Nurse, but her mind is elsewhere. She tells the Nurse that she wants to sleep alone tonight (in the past the two have shared a bed). Lady Capulet comes to wish her goodnight, as well. Juliet bids her two mother figures goodnight, knowing that it's actually a permanent goodbye. She longs to call them back, but at last steels herself:

> Farewell.—God knows when we shall meet again.
> I have a faint cold fear thrills through my veins
> That almost freezes up the heat of life.
> I'll call them back again to comfort me.
> Nurse!—What should she do here?
> My dismal scene I needs must act alone.
> Come, vial (4.3.15-21).

She thinks aloud, wondering if Friar Lawrence might actually be poisoning her to keep from being dishonored— she has learned not to trust the adults in her life. She talks herself out of this paranoia, and instead imagines the horrors she may encounter in the tomb: What if she suffocates, or what if the gruesome sight and smell of the corpses around her drives her mad? At last, she overcomes her terror, and drains the vial: "Romeo, Romeo, Romeo! Here's drink. I drink to thee" (4.3.60).

Act IV, Scene 4 Summary

Lady Capulet, Lord Capulet, and the Nurse are bustling around preparing for Juliet's wedding morning. The Nurse warns Lord Capulet that he's going to make himself sick staying up all night. Lord Capulet, waving her off, tells her to go and wake Juliet so she can start getting ready.

Act IV, Scene 5 Summary

The Nurse arrives in Juliet's bedroom and tries to wake her with some of her usual dirty jokes: "Sleep for a week, for the next night, I warrant,/The county Paris hath set up his rest/That you shall rest but little" (4.5.6-8). Of course, Juliet doesn't wake. The screaming Nurse summons Lord and Lady Capulet, who fall into shock.

Friar Lawrence arrives to conduct the marriage, bringing Paris with him. The family and the bridegroom all mourn violently over Juliet's body. Friar Lawrence scolds them for their excesses:

> Your part in her you could not keep from death,
> But heaven keeps his part in eternal life.
> The most you sought was her promotion,
> For 'twas your heaven she should be advanced;
> And weep you now, seeing she is advanced
> Above the clouds, as high as heaven itself? (4.5.75-80)

Lord Capulet turns all the wedding preparations into funeral preparations. The scene ends incongruously with bickering musicians making musical puns—less worried about a child's death than getting paid.

Act V, Scene 1 Summary

Romeo, in Mantua, has had another dream, this time a good one: "If I may trust the flattering truth of sleep,/My dreams presage some joyful news at hand" (5.1.1-2). He recalls his dream, in which Juliet found him dead, kissed him, and revived him to joy. However, his hopeful thoughts are interrupted when his servant Balthazar delivers news from Verona: Juliet is dead. Romeo bewails his fate, railing against the stars. He tells Balthazar to fetch him a horse. Balthazar tries to calm him down, telling him not to do anything rash, but Romeo insists. Left to himself, he begins to plan his own suicide.

An apothecary wandering around town looks to have fallen on hard times; it's illegal to sell poison, but Romeo bets he can persuade this man to do it. This same Apothecary happens to be passing by, and Romeo asks him for "a dram of poison, such soon-speeding gear/As will disperse itself through all the veins,/That the life-weary taker may fall dead" (5.1.64-66). The desperate apothecary agrees to sell him poison. Romeo takes his deadly vial and hurries to Verona.

Act V, Scene 2 Summary

Friar Lawrence is hailed by another monk, Friar John—the man whom he sent to Mantua to deliver the details of his plan to Romeo. Friar John was held up by an anti-plague quarantine and could not deliver the message. Friar Lawrence, in a panic, tells Friar John to get him a crowbar: He's going to break into the Capulet tomb, rescue Juliet when she awakes, and intercept Romeo.

Act V, Scene 3 Summary

Paris has arrived at the Capulet family tomb to pay his respects to Juliet. He scatters flowers over the tomb, and vows to mourn there. However, at the sound of approaching footsteps, he hides himself. Romeo arrives with Balthazar, and the two break into the tomb. Romeo tells Balthazar that he's just there to look on Juliet's face and to take an important ring from her finger, and warns him to go away and never speak of what he's seen. Balthazar, frightened, agrees, but quietly plans to stay and watch; he's worried for Romeo.

Paris steps out from the shadows and challenges Romeo, believing him to be here to desecrate the Capulet grave. Romeo tries to peacefully send him away, but Paris resists. The two men fight, and Romeo kills Paris; Paris's last wish is to be buried next to Juliet. Romeo drags the body into the tomb. There, he finds Juliet. He mourns over her body, noting that death seems to have had no effect on her beauty:

> Death, that has sucked the honey of thy breath,
> Hath had no power yet upon thy beauty.
> Thou art not conquered. Beauty's ensign yet
> Is crimson in thy lips and in thy cheeks (5.3.92-95).

Vowing to stay here with Juliet forever, he gives her a last kiss, toasts her with poison, and falls: "Here's to my love. O true apothecary,/Thy drugs are quick. Thus with a kiss I die" (5.3.119-20). Only just too late, Friar Lawrence arrives and finds Balthazar outside the tomb. Balthazar tells him as much as he knows, and Friar Lawrence descends into the tomb. There he finds the bodies of Paris and Romeo, and Juliet, just waking up. Friar Lawrence tries to hurry Juliet away, eager to hide any evidence of his own involvement.

He can hear the night watch approaching, and insists that they get out of there as quickly as possible:

> Come, come away.
> Thy husband in thy bosom there lies dead,
> And Paris, too. Come, I'll dispose of thee
> Among a sisterhood of holy nuns (5.3.159-62).

However, Juliet is having none of it and refuses to leave. Friar Lawrence, panicking, abandons her. Juliet, alone, examines Romeo's dead body, finding the poison vial, and discovering that his lips are still warm. The watch is at the door of the tomb, now. She takes Romeo's dagger and stabs herself to death.

The watch arrives and discovers all the bodies. They summon the Prince and the Montague and Capulet families, though Lady Montague has died of grief over Romeo's exile. Friar Lawrence, with the corroboration of Balthazar, explains what has happened to the assembled crowd. The grieving Lord Capulet and Lord Montague take each other's hands and vow to end their feud and to erect statues of Romeo and Juliet in Verona. The Prince ends the play, promising that "Some shall be pardoned, and some punished./For never was a story of more woe/Than this of Juliet and her Romeo" (5.3.319-21).

Acts IV-V Analysis

Shakespeare forces his audience to consider the uncomfortably close relationship between love and death. The play's gorgeous celestial imagery takes on a darker tone: The night that brings the lovers together has a lot in common with the blackness of a tomb populated with horrors.

The doubts and fears of the earlier acts come together in the young lovers' inexorable approach to their deaths. As Juliet prepares to go through with the plan that she believes will lead to her reunion with Romeo, she has queasy visions of the horrors of the tomb: She vividly imagines "loathsome smells" and Tybalt "festering in his shroud" (4.3.44-47). Even as she imagines finally consummating her love with Romeo, Juliet thinks of death:

> Give me my Romeo; and, when I shall die,
> Take him and cut him out in little stars,
> And he will make the face of heaven so fine
> That all the world will be in love with night
> And pay no worship to the garish sun (3.2.23-27).

Here, the linkage between love and death is most clear. To "die" was sometimes a metaphor for orgasm: There's a sense that Juliet's experience of sexuality has in it the same loss of self that death brings. That loss of self comes equally to Romeo in this image: His imagined death makes him into the stars—beautiful, but no longer himself.

As noted in the Analysis section for Act III, Mercutio's death helps to make death real in the play's world. Acts IV and V drive that reality home through the poignant youth of the characters who die (of the young, only Benvolio is left standing). In a world founded on the power of fancy and imagination, death comes as the ultimate rejoinder. It has in it both the mystery of dreams and the awesome power of finality: Whatever death is, it isn't a fantasy.

Juliet

Juliet is the 13-year-old only daughter of Lord and Lady Capulet. Slated to marry Count Paris, she instead falls in love with the scion of the Capulets' enemies, Romeo Montague.

The youngest and most seemingly innocent character of the play is also its boldest, most serious, and (in an odd way) most sensible. Juliet is just as passionate and just as love-struck as Romeo, but her love stays a little more grounded: While Romeo is talking about the wings of love, she's wondering how on earth he climbed her high garden wall. She's also thoughtful about the changeability and dangers of love, even as she is carried away by her feelings for Romeo.

Throughout the play, Juliet demonstrates tremendous bravery and loyalty. As the adults around her reveal that they are no less fickle, irrational, and violent than the young, she stays loyal to herself, and is willing to undergo real terrors for the sake of her love.

Romeo

Romeo is the only son of Lord and Lady Montague, who are engaged in an endless feud with the Capulets. After falling madly in love with Juliet, Romeo marries her in secret and then kills himself under the mistaken impression that she has died.

Romeo is the very picture of the Renaissance lover: He's passionate, moody, melancholy, and impulsive. While at the beginning of the play he's assuring everyone that he'll pine forever over the inaccessible Rosaline, he falls deeply in love with Juliet the moment he sees her. However, his name suggests a religious pilgrim (one on his way to Rome): There's true devotion in him as well as unmanaged passion.

Romeo's passion is at once sincere and dangerous. He's willing to put himself in danger for the sake of love, and happy to agree to an immediate marriage—but as Juliet herself often notes, he's changeable.

While Romeo is mutable, his feelings are sincere. He truly loves and is loyal to his friends, who tease him relentlessly about his amours. In the end, his love, like Juliet's, is powerful enough to drive him to his death. He embodies both the beauties and the dangers of youthful passion.

Mercutio

The flamboyant, virtuosic, and (appropriately) mercurial Mercutio plays a critical role in *Romeo and Juliet*. While at first he might seem tangential to the main action—he's neither a Montague nor a Capulet—his death marks the play's transition from a comedy to a tragedy.

Mercutio is deeply attached to Romeo, and spends a lot of time trying to snap his melancholic friend out of his moping. His outward approach to the world is to take nothing seriously; he's an inveterate punner who loves the slipperiness of language. However, he often seems inwardly disturbed by this slipperiness. For instance, his description of Queen Mab moves from sly joking to a fearful account of a "hag" who rapes sleeping women. This speech, which describes the terrifying power of dreams, points at Mercutio's importance: He, perhaps more than anyone else in the play, is able to see that dreams and fantasies have real and dangerous consequences.

Nurse

The Nurse is Juliet's closest friend and caretaker. While Juliet's real mother is distant and formal, the Nurse is anything but. Unstoppably talkative and deeply affectionate, she has a taste for ribald jokes and has a lighthearted view of the world. She supports and enables Juliet's impulsive marriage to Romeo because she is a romantic and because she loves Juliet.

This sincere affection, however, doesn't extend to an understanding of Juliet's real depth of feeling. For the Nurse, romantic love is mostly just a sexual impulse; she counsels Juliet to give up on Romeo after he flees to Mantua and marry Paris for his looks. The Nurse exemplifies the limits of many of the characters' strictly sexual readings of love.

Benvolio

Benvolio, like Mercutio and Romeo, has a significant name: He only has good (*ben*) wishes (*volio*). A natural peacekeeper and a gentle soul, he tempers Romeo's passion and Mercutio's spontaneity. However, urge pragmatism and down-to-earth behavior often can't overcome the sheer power of human passion; his efforts to break up fights often make things worse. At the end of the play, he's the only young man of the Montague family left alive.

Tybalt

Tybalt is Juliet's hot-blooded cousin. Mercutio heaps scorn on Tybalt's affected fighting style, but he's a dangerous opponent, known for his love of quarreling in the street. Tybalt is often referred to as the "prince of cats," as he shares a name with a legendary archetypal cat character in a popular sequence of fables. Like his feline namesake, he is prideful, solitary, and deadly. His loyalty to his own family is a cover for his own egotism and aggression: When his uncle won't give in to Tybalt's desire to fight Romeo at the Capulet feast, Tybalt's pride spurs him to take the revenge that sets the play's final tragedies in motion. He is, however, much loved by his household, and the Nurse remembers him as a friend.

Friar Lawrence

Friar Lawrence is Romeo's counterpart to Juliet's Nurse. A father figure to an impulsive boy, Friar Lawrence counsels temperance and moderation where the Nurse encourages a lusty embrace of the appetites. However, the Friar's philosophy leads him to the same half-baked decisions as the Nurse's, and to a similar ultimate disloyalty. At first, he abets the young lovers' secret marriage; in the end, he abandons Juliet to her suicide.

Like the Nurse, Friar Lawrence demonstrates the limits of rationality and cool-headedness, which can't defeat the power of the feelings or the vagaries of chance.

The Beauty and Danger of Love

Modern readers often think of *Romeo and Juliet* as the "love play," to the extent that we still use the young couple's names as a byword for head-over-heels couples. However, this play is as much about love's illusions, deceptions, and dangers as much as its beauties.

Every character in the play knows that the intensity of new love can be "more inconstant than the wind" (1.4.107). The power of Romeo and Juliet's love is beautifully and vividly drawn, but it emerges from a background of utter silliness. Romeo's rapid flip from believing he shall never love anyone the way he loves Rosaline (who wants nothing to do with him) to having eyes for no one but Juliet is emblematic of a teenager in love. Romeo's friends never let him forget that he's being ridiculous, but they can't hold him back.

The beauty and the danger of love is that it can be ridiculous and real at the same time—and that it has a power that goes far deeper than reason. Juliet is perhaps the best spokeswoman for this theme. Though she remains aware that the intensity of her feeling is dangerous and likely to vanish as soon as it appears, "too like the lightning" (2.2.26), she doesn't let that stop her from being carried away by it—and indeed, perhaps she can't.

The imagery of love in *Romeo and Juliet* often features huge, impersonal, beautiful, and fateful forces: the sun, the moon, and the stars. (See "Symbols and Motifs" for further discussion of the play's celestial imagery.) If love is like these things, it is not only awe-inspiring, but a controller of destinies. Friar Lawrence might urge temperance around love, and the Nurse might boil it down to pure sex, but who can resist the pull of the stars?

Dreams and Illusions

Romeo and Juliet contains three powerful dreams. Two are Romeo's, and one is Mercutio's.

At the outset of the play, Romeo has an ominous dream of death just before he meets Juliet for the first time; at the end, he dreams a beautiful dream of resurrection just before he kills himself in despair. Both of these dreams are, in their way, truthful, but the way they align with reality is not obvious to the characters from their position within the play.

Mercutio spins his dream—that "dreamers often lie" (1.4.55)—into a disturbing fairy tale: his great Queen Mab speech about the nature of visions. In it, he enumerates how this sinister fairy queen distributes dreams appropriate to their dreamers: Lovers dream of love, lawyers dream of fees, and so on. However, the Queen also hands out punishments and suffering, leaving behind sores and blisters, even deflowering sleeping girls like a succubus.

Dreams, *Romeo and Juliet* suggests, have their own reality, their own weight, and their own dangers. Human experience, even the most powerful, has in it an element of fantasy; we see through the lens of our dreams, and are controlled by forces beyond our conscious understanding.

Rivalry and Feud

Romeo and Juliet is famously a story of warring families, and many modern adaptations of the play focus on that rivalry. Within the play, the danger of the feud between the

Montagues and Capulets is not that it's bleak and violent, but that it's silly: It's only made serious by terrible accidents. We don't learn the origin of the vendetta, which seems so old and rote that there's a degree of fun in continuing it. When the Montagues and the Capulets fight in the street, there's playfulness in their punny sparring. Lord Capulet is willing to turn a blind eye when Romeo crashes his party, and reports approvingly that the young man "bears him like a portly gentleman" (1.5.75); he's even willing, after being scolded by the Prince, to try to keep the peace with his hated enemy, Lord Montague.

In short, though this feud springs from a genuine grudge, it is as much a matter of habit as of active hatred. It's notable that the feud only breaks into serious violence after Lord Capulet scolds and shames Tybalt; since Tybalt can't take out his wounded pride on his uncle, he turns against Romeo instead. When Romeo refuses to fight Tybalt, Mercutio and not a Montague leaps to his defense—loyal to Romeo as a friend, not a kinsman.

Clan loyalty is a fantasy and an excuse, not a true motivation. Juliet wonders, "What's in a name?" (2.2.46)— perhaps, it is a cover for one's deeper, darker, and more personal fears, hates, and grudges.

Celestial Bodies

The beautiful and impersonal forces of the heavens are a constant note in *Romeo and Juliet*. From Romeo's first impassioned speech in which "Juliet is the sun" (2.2.3) to Juliet's "take him and cut him out in little stars" (3.2.22), the lovers see each other in celestial terms. These images will make perfect sense to anyone who's ever been head-over-heels in love: A beloved person indeed seems to shine, just as the sun and stars do.

However, the lovers run into trouble when they talk about the moon. Associated with both virginity and changeability, the moon holds both Romeo and Juliet's deepest fears: Romeo that Juliet will deny him, Juliet that Romeo will fall out of love with her as easily as he fell into love with her.

As well as their beauty, the stars play the role of fate. At the very beginning of the play, the Chorus tells us that these are "star-crossed lovers" (1.Prologue.6): Lovers whose ultimate doom was spelled out in the stars before they even met. (See more on this motif below.)

The symbolic weight of the sun, moon, and stars is comparable to the roles that day and night play in the story. Romeo and Juliet can almost never be together by the light of day. When they poignantly argue over whether the bird they're hearing is a nightingale or a lark, they point to one of the play's great sadnesses: Their love never sees the bright, certain light of the sun. In its celestial imagery as in so much else, *Romeo and Juliet* explores the paradoxes of love.

Medicines and Poisons

When we first meet Friar Lawrence, he's cutting herbs in his garden, musing on their powers. A medicinal plant, he reflects, can do as much evil as good, if abused; a poisonous herb, meanwhile, can have healthy effects if dosed correctly. It's all a matter of how you use them. He goes on to add that it's much the same with people:

> Two such opposed kings encamp them still
> In man as well as herbs—grace and rude will;
> And where the worser is predominant,
> Full soon the canker death eats up that plant (2.3.28-31).

A plant is like a person in that its virtues can easily turn into vices, and vice-versa. While the warning about "the canker death" seems plainly to foreshadow the passion-driven demise of Romeo and Juliet, Friar Lawrence's ideal of moderation is also hard to meet, and doesn't stop him from ending up outside a tomb with a crowbar in the middle of the night.

Juliet's sleeping potion and Romeo's poison appear in very similar guises, and the two lovers go through a similar process of working themselves up to drink their final drinks—even toasting each other across space and time as a last shared act. While Juliet's potion only makes her sleep, this hardly matters: In the end, it's not the nature of the drug, but all the forces around it, that determine whether she lives or dies. Friar Lawrence's sleeping potion is, in the end, no less an agent of tragedy than Romeo's real poison. Human efforts to moderate have only so much power against the vagaries of fate.

Fate

The opening lines of the play let us know that we're going to hear a tale of "star-cross'd lovers" (1.Prologue.6). A Renaissance audience would know that these were the stars of destiny itself. Though there were certainly skeptics (see Act I, Scene 2 of *King Lear* for an example), people took astrology seriously, and many believed that the disposition of the stars and planets at one's birth had a genuine influence over one's fate.

Fate, as represented by the stars, is both inexorable and mysterious. Throughout the play, we see human hopes and dreams dashed by coincidence and accident, and dreams giving true (if murky) pictures of what's to come. No one's plan works out in this world: or, if it does, it leads to unintended and terrible consequences. The ending is set from the beginning, no matter what anyone does.

Romeo is quick to see the workings of fate in these unhappy accidents, crying, "then I deny you, stars!" (5.1.25), at the news of Juliet's death. (Note that some versions have the line as "defy" rather than "deny"—this is all part of the fun of trying to establish an authoritative Shakespeare text.) Whether it's "deny" or "defy," the wish to strike out at fate here motivates Romeo to bring about something very like the fate he's trying to defy.

From the very beginning of the play, the audience knows what's going to happen: The Prologue tells us almost the whole plot. The play creates tension by showing us *how* the tragedies come about, leading us to consider the forces that act in our world, without our knowing and beyond our control. Who is the author of reality? Certainly not humans—or, at least, not humans alone.

1. "Two households, both alike in dignity,
    In fair Verona, where we lay our scene,
    From ancient grudge break to new mutiny,
    Where civil blood makes civil hands unclean.
    From forth the fatal loins of these two foes
    A pair of star-cross'd lovers take their life;
    Whose misadventured piteous overthrows
    Do with their death bury their parents' strife.
    The fearful passage of their death-mark'd love,
    And the continuance of their parents' rage,
    Which, but their children's end, nought could remove,
    Is now the two hours' traffic of our stage;
    The which if you with patient ears attend,
    What here shall miss, our toil shall strive to mend."
    (Act I, Prologue, Lines 1-14)

    The Prologue provides a complete overview of the play,
    including its tragic ending. Spelling out what is going
    to happen points to an important theme of the play—
    human actions often seem out of human control.
    Chance and uncontrollable impulse push the characters
    to their fates. Is what happens in this play indeed
    written in the stars? Notably, this Prologue is a sonnet,
    a form that will become important throughout the play
    (see Romeo and Juliet's first meeting, below).

2. "GREGORY
    To move is to stir; and to be valiant is to stand:
    therefore, if thou art moved, thou runn'st away.
    SAMPSON
    A dog of that house shall move me to stand: I
    will
    take the wall of any man or maid of Montague's.
    GREGORY

That shows thee a weak slave; for the weakest
goes
to the wall.
SAMPSON
True; and therefore women, being the weaker
vessels,
are ever thrust to the wall: therefore I will push
Montague's men from the wall, and thrust his
maids
to the wall.
GREGORY
The quarrel is between our masters and us their
men.
SAMPSON
'Tis all one, I will show myself a tyrant: when I
have fought with the men, I will be cruel with the
maids, and cut off their heads.
GREGORY
The heads of the maids?
SAMPSON
Ay, the heads of the maids, or their maidenheads;
take it in what sense thou wilt.
GREGORY
They must take it in sense that feel it.
SAMPSON
Me they shall feel while I am able to stand: and
'tis known I am a pretty piece of flesh.
GREGORY
'Tis well thou art not fish; if thou hadst, thou
hadst been poor John. Draw thy tool! here comes
two of the house of the Montagues.
SAMPSON
My naked weapon is out: quarrel, I will back
thee." (Act I, Scene 1, Lines 9-35)

This lengthy sequence of ribald puns is our first taste of Verona. From it, we learn a great deal about this world. It's a place full of impulsive young men showing off, and a place where words don't always mean what they seem to mean. Sexuality, violence, and ego are all present in this ever-building string of sex jokes.

3. "Here's much to do with hate, though more with love.
    Why then, O brawling love, O loving hate,
    O anything of nothing first create!
    O heavy lightness, serious vanity,
    Misshapen chaos of well-seeming forms,
    Feather of lead, bright smoke, cold fire, sick health,
    Still-waking sleep that is not what it is!
    This love feel I, that feel no love in this.
    Dost thou not laugh?" (Act I, Scene 1, Lines 180-88)

    Romeo's lengthy reflection on the paradoxes of love is at once prescient and a little ridiculous. He's right in noting the difficulties of love—that it can be at once tormenting and beautiful, absurd and deadly serious— and all these truths will come into play soon. However, he's also addressing the sensible and peace-loving Benvolio, who, while he claims a line later to be weeping over Romeo's suffering, seems to be at least suppressing a little smile here. Romeo's reflections on the difficulties of love can't make him see that he is both truly sad and goofy.

4. "And she was wean'd,—I never shall forget it,—
    Of all the days of the year, upon that day:
    For I had then laid wormwood to my dug,
    Sitting in the sun under the dove-house wall;

My lord and you were then at Mantua:—
Nay, I do bear a brain:—but, as I said,
When it did taste the wormwood on the nipple
Of my dug and felt it bitter, pretty fool,
To see it tetchy and fall out with the dug!
Shake quoth the dove-house: 'twas no need, I trow,
To bid me trudge:
And since that time it is eleven years;
For then she could stand alone; nay, by the rood,
She could have run and waddled all about;
For even the day before, she broke her brow:
And then my husband—God be with his soul!
A' was a merry man—took up the child:
'Yea,' quoth he, 'dost thou fall upon thy face?
Thou wilt fall backward when thou hast more wit;
Wilt thou not, Jule?' and, by my holidame,
The pretty wretch left crying and said 'Ay.'
To see, now, how a jest shall come about!
I warrant, an I should live a thousand years,
I never should forget it: 'Wilt thou not, Jule?' quoth he;
And, pretty fool, it stinted and said 'Ay.'" (Act I, Scene
3, Lines 26-52)

The Nurse's garrulous speech introduces us to another
side of sex, love, and family in Verona. Juliet's own
mother is chilly and formal with her daughter, but the
Nurse is a fount of reminiscences and bawdy humor.
Here, the Nurse affectionately remembers Juliet's
childhood and her dead husband, who seemed to like a
good dirty joke as much as the Nurse does. There's a
female side of Verona's sexual coin that's just as rude
and as bodily as the male, under all the formalities of
marriage contracts and social status.

5. "O, then, I see Queen Mab hath been with you.
   She is the fairies' midwife, and she comes

In shape no bigger than an agate-stone
On the fore-finger of an alderman,
Drawn with a team of little atomies
Athwart men's noses as they lie asleep;
Her wagon-spokes made of long spiders' legs,
The cover of the wings of grasshoppers,
The traces of the smallest spider's web,
The collars of the moonshine's watery beams,
Her whip of cricket's bone, the lash of film,
Her wagoner a small grey-coated gnat,
Not so big as a round little worm
Prick'd from the lazy finger of a maid;
Her chariot is an empty hazel-nut
Made by the joiner squirrel or old grub,
Time out o' mind the fairies' coachmakers.
And in this state she gallops night by night
Through lovers' brains, and then they dream of
love;
O'er courtiers' knees, that dream on court'sies
straight,
O'er lawyers' fingers, who straight dream on
fees,
O'er ladies' lips, who straight on kisses dream,
Which oft the angry Mab with blisters plagues,
Because their breaths with sweetmeats tainted
are:
Sometime she gallops o'er a courtier's nose,
And then dreams he of smelling out a suit;
And sometime comes she with a tithe-pig's tail
Tickling a parson's nose as a' lies asleep,
Then dreams, he of another benefice:
Sometime she driveth o'er a soldier's neck,
And then dreams he of cutting foreign throats,
Of breaches, ambuscadoes, Spanish blades,
Of healths five-fathom deep; and then anon
Drums in his ear, at which he starts and wakes,

And being thus frighted swears a prayer or two
And sleeps again. This is that very Mab
That plats the manes of horses in the night,
And bakes the elflocks in foul sluttish hairs,
Which once untangled, much misfortune bodes:
This is the hag, when maids lie on their backs,
That presses them and learns them first to bear,
Making them women of good carriage:
This is she—" (Act I, Scene 4, Lines 58-100)

*Mercutio's virtuosic Queen Mab speech tells us a lot
about both Mercutio and the world he lives in. Mercutio
is a brilliant talker, and one who doesn't seem to take
much of anything seriously. He lives between the world
of the Montagues and the Capulets, hanging out with
Romeo and getting invited to Lord Capulet's parties.
Here, he envisions another sort of between: the world
of dreams, whose ruler is the mischievous Queen Mab.
The speech gets increasingly sinister. At first, Mab
delivers the dreams one would expect, then she starts
handing out punishments, until she's a messenger of
both doom and of nightmarish sexuality. Dreams, which
Mercutio wants to present as meaningless, are in fact
deadly serious.*

6. "ROMEO
   If I profane with my unworthiest hand
   This holy shrine, the gentle fine is this:
   My lips, two blushing pilgrims, ready stand
   To smooth that rough touch with a tender kiss.
   JULIET
   Good pilgrim, you do wrong your hand too much,
   Which mannerly devotion shows in this;
   For saints have hands that pilgrims' hands do
   touch,
   And palm to palm is holy palmers' kiss.

ROMEO
Have not saints lips, and holy palmers too?
JULIET
Ay, pilgrim, lips that they must use in prayer.
ROMEO
O, then, dear saint, let lips do what hands do;
They pray, grant thou, lest faith turn to despair.
JULIET
Saints do not move, though grant for prayers'
sake.
ROMEO
Then move not, while my prayer's effect I take.
Thus from my lips, by yours, my sin is purged.
JULIET
Then have my lips the sin that they have took.
ROMEO
Sin from thy lips? O trespass sweetly urged!
Give me my sin again.
JULIET
You kiss by the book." (Act I, Scene 5, Lines
104-22)

Romeo and Juliet's first encounter takes the form of a sonnet. The two young lovers trade rhyming lines, building a poem. In typical fashion, this sonnet works out a problem. Romeo desires a kiss as a pilgrimage, but Juliet points out that pilgrims' lips are for praying. In response, Romeo notes that pilgrims touch the hands of holy statues of saints, so one could imagine lips doing the same. At last, the two imagine their kiss as passing "sin" back and forth. Love unites what is holy with what is profane, similar to Romeo's earlier musings on the paradoxes of love.

7. "He jests at scars that never felt a wound.

But, soft! what light through yonder window
breaks?
It is the east, and Juliet is the sun.
Arise, fair sun, and kill the envious moon,
Who is already sick and pale with grief,
That thou her maid art far more fair than she:
Be not her maid, since she is envious;
Her vestal livery is but sick and green
And none but fools do wear it; cast it off.
It is my lady, O, it is my love!
O, that she knew she were!
She speaks yet she says nothing: what of that?
Her eye discourses; I will answer it.
I am too bold, 'tis not to me she speaks:
Two of the fairest stars in all the heaven,
Having some business, do entreat her eyes
To twinkle in their spheres till they return.
What if her eyes were there, they in her head?
The brightness of her cheek would shame those
stars,
As daylight doth a lamp; her eyes in heaven
Would through the airy region stream so bright
That birds would sing and think it were not night.
See, how she leans her cheek upon her hand!
O, that I were a glove upon that hand,
That I might touch that cheek!" (Act II, Scene 2,
Lines 1-26)

*Romeo's famous speech establishes the passion
between these two love-struck teenagers and some of
the play's most persistent images. Romeo and Juliet
often imagine each other as celestial bodies, especially
the stars and the sun. When Romeo imagines Juliet as
the sun, he's seeing her as not only a gorgeous light,
but also the source of life itself. Keep an eye on their
use of the moon: Both often forswear the moon; it's too*

inconstant, too changeable, and too virginal for comfort.

8. "What's in a name? That which we call a rose
By any other word would smell as sweet." (Act II,
Scene 2, Lines 46-47)

In her (she believes) private musings on Romeo, Juliet reflects that a name is not the essential part of a thing: A word is only a gesture at the reality. What's true of Romeo is not that he is a Montague, but that he is himself. This is a different spin on the slipperiness of language: Here, Juliet places her faith in a reality that is past words.

9. "Well, do not swear: although I joy in thee,
I have no joy of this contract to-night:
It is too rash, too unadvised, too sudden;
Too like the lightning, which doth cease to be
Ere one can say 'It lightens.' Sweet, good night!
This bud of love, by summer's ripening breath,
May prove a beauteous flower when next we
meet.
Good night, good night! as sweet repose and rest
Come to thy heart as that within my breast!" (Act
II, Scene 2, Lines 123-31)

Though Romeo often imagines Juliet as the sun or the stars or a soaring angel, Juliet keeps her feet more firmly planted on the ground. Though by the end of this scene she's telling Romeo that she'll marry him tomorrow, here, she is able to see their overwhelming passion as not merely rapturous, but dangerous. When she cautions Romeo not to swear by the moon, and then not to swear on anything, she's being both pragmatic and superstitious: A love so strong and immediate is

both hard to believe in and almost impossible not to be
swept up by.

10. "O, mickle is the powerful grace that lies
    In herbs, plants, stones, and their true qualities:
    For nought so vile that on the earth doth live
    But to the earth some special good doth give,
    Nor aught so good but strain'd from that fair use
    Revolts from true birth, stumbling on abuse:
    Virtue itself turns vice, being misapplied;
    And vice sometimes by action dignified.
    Within the infant rind of this small flower
    Poison hath residence and medicine power:
    For this, being smelt, with that part cheers each
    part;
    Being tasted, slays all senses with the heart.
    Two such opposed kings encamp them still
    In man as well as herbs, grace and rude will;
    And where the worser is predominant,
    Full soon the canker death eats up that plant."
    (Act II, Scene 3, Lines 15-22)

Friar Lawrence's speech on the contradictory
properties of herbs and the virtue of moderation
introduces us to some of the contradictions of his own
character. In spite of his sensible approach, and his
understanding that good and bad come as much from
context and application as from any inherent property
of a thing, all of his efforts to moderate and ameliorate
according to these principles will end in tragedy. Friar
Lawrence understands the power of nature, but he's
mistaken in thinking he can harness that power through
reason alone.

11. "JULIET
    I' faith, I am sorry that thou art not well.

Sweet, sweet, sweet nurse, tell me, what says my
love?
NURSE
Your love says, like an honest gentleman, and a
courteous, and a kind, and a handsome, and, I
warrant, a virtuous,—Where is your mother?
JULIET
Where is my mother! why, she is within;
Where should she be? How oddly thou repliest!
'Your love says, like an honest gentleman,
Where is your mother?'" (Act II, Scene 5, Lines
56-65)

*This comical exchange between the Nurse and Juliet—
Juliet impatient for the most important news of her life,
the Nurse distractible and self-absorbed—is not only an
example of the relationship between the two, but an
image of the divide between the old and the young.
Even the sex-obsessed Nurse can't quite understand
how urgent news of Romeo is to Juliet. This adult
incomprehension, this sense that Juliet's real feelings
are silly, will return tragically when the Nurse counsels
Juliet to go ahead and marry Paris.*

12. "ROMEO
Courage, man; the hurt cannot be much.
MERCUTIO
No, 'tis not so deep as a well, nor so wide as a
church-door; but 'tis enough, 'twill serve: ask for
me to-morrow, and you shall find me a grave
man. I
am peppered, I warrant, for this world. A plague
o'
both your houses! 'Zounds, a dog, a rat, a mouse,
a
cat, to scratch a man to death! a braggart, a

rogue, a villain, that fights by the book of
arithmetic! Why the devil came you between us?
I
was hurt under your arm.
ROMEO
I thought all for the best.
MERCUTIO
Help me into some house, Benvolio,
Or I shall faint. A plague o' both your houses!
They have made worms' meat of me: I have it,
And soundly too: your houses!" (Act III, Scene 1,
Lines 99-113)

*Mercutio dies as he lived: punning. His death sets in
motion the mechanism of the final tragedy and points to
one of the play's big themes. When Mercutio asks
Romeo why he came between him and Tybalt, giving
Tybalt the chance to fatally wound him, Romeo replies
that he was just trying to do what he thought was best.
However, human ideas about what is best have only so
much power next to the massive force of chance,
accident, and passion.*

13. "Gallop apace, you fiery-footed steeds,
    Towards Phoebus' lodging: such a wagoner
    As Phaethon would whip you to the west,
    And bring in cloudy night immediately.
    Spread thy close curtain, love-performing night,
    That runaway's eyes may wink and Romeo
    Leap to these arms, untalk'd of and unseen.
    Lovers can see to do their amorous rites
    By their own beauties; or, if love be blind,
    It best agrees with night. Come, civil night,
    Thou sober-suited matron, all in black,
    And learn me how to lose a winning match,
    Play'd for a pair of stainless maidenhoods:

Hood my unmann'd blood, bating in my cheeks,
With thy black mantle; till strange love, grown bold,
Think true love acted simple modesty.
Come, night; come, Romeo; come, thou day in night;
For thou wilt lie upon the wings of night
Whiter than new snow on a raven's back.
Come, gentle night, come, loving, black-brow'd night,
Give me my Romeo; and, when he shall die,
Take him and cut him out in little stars,
And he will make the face of heaven so fine
That all the world will be in love with night
And pay no worship to the garish sun.
O, I have bought the mansion of a love,
But not possess'd it, and, though I am sold,
Not yet enjoy'd: so tedious is this day
As is the night before some festival
To an impatient child that hath new robes
And may not wear them." (Act III, Scene 2, Lines 1-33)

Juliet's speech of longing is laden with dramatic irony. She, unlike the audience, does not yet know that the Prince has banished Romeo, and her gorgeous language is thus painfully poignant. As ever, Juliet imagines her love in the context of day and night, sun and moon. She wishes for the darkness of night to come and shelter her and Romeo—and indeed, their love will never see the light of day.

14. "O serpent heart hid with a flow'ring face!
    Did ever dragon keep so fair a cave?
    Beautiful tyrant, fiend angelical!
    Dove-feathered raven, wolvish-ravening lamb!

Despisèd substance of divinest show!
Just opposite to what thou justly seem'st,
A damnèd saint, an honorable villain.
O nature, what hadst thou to do in hell
When thou didst bower the spirit of a fiend
In mortal paradise of such sweet flesh?
Was ever book containing such vile matter
So fairly bound? O, that deceit should dwell
In such a gorgeous palace!" (Act III, Scene 2,
Lines 79-91)

As Juliet mourns Romeo slaying Tybalt, her words recapitulate earlier speeches. Benvolio once told Romeo he'd find him a girl who made Rosaline look like a crow next to a dove—an image of blackness and whiteness that Romeo repeats when he first sees Juliet. Juliet now sees Romeo's beautiful exterior hiding a dark inside. The book metaphor her mother used to describe Paris also reappears here. In this moment, Juliet is seeing that the reality sometimes doesn't just flip back and forth between extremes—instead, the extremes coexist in the same place.

15. "JULIET
Wilt thou be gone? it is not yet near day:
It was the nightingale, and not the lark,
That pierced the fearful hollow of thine ear;
Nightly she sings on yon pomegranate-tree:
Believe me, love, it was the nightingale.
ROMEO
It was the lark, the herald of the morn,
No nightingale: look, love, what envious streaks
Do lace the severing clouds in yonder east:
Night's candles are burnt out, and jocund day
Stands tiptoe on the misty mountain tops.

I must be gone and live, or stay and die." (Act III, Scene 5, Lines 1-11)

On the morning after their wedding night, Romeo and Juliet must prepare themselves for a painful parting. Yet again, we encounter the importance of interpretation: Juliet wishes, at first, to pretend that the lark they hear heralding the morning is in fact a nightingale. Later, Romeo, at first realistic, will make this same claim, and it will be Juliet who insists he needs to listen to the lark and get out of here before he's executed. Fantasy, dreams, and the power of longing transform experience—until they collide with an immovable reality.

16. "JULIET
O think'st thou we shall ever meet again?
ROMEO
I doubt it not; and all these woes shall serve
For sweet discourses in our time to come.
JULIET
O God, I have an ill-divining soul!
Methinks I see thee, now thou art below,
As one dead in the bottom of a tomb:
Either my eyesight fails, or thou look'st pale."
(Act III, Scene 5, Lines 51-57)

During their poignant farewell, Juliet has a vision not unlike Romeo's at the beginning of the play. Looking down from the same balcony where the two first declared their love, Juliet sees Romeo as if he's already dead and entombed. Romeo's brave assertion that they'll laugh about all this later points at the play's one thread of hope: Romeo dreams of Juliet's kiss resurrecting him—a hint of a heavenly reunion, if not an earthly one.

17. "LADY CAPULET
Marry, my child, early next Thursday morn,
The gallant, young and noble gentleman,
The County Paris, at Saint Peter's Church,
Shall happily make thee there a joyful bride.
JULIET
Now, by Saint Peter's Church and Peter too,
He shall not make me there a joyful bride.
I wonder at this haste; that I must wed
Ere he, that should be husband, comes to woo.
I pray you, tell my lord and father, madam,
I will not marry yet; and, when I do, I swear,
It shall be Romeo, whom you know I hate,
Rather than Paris. These are news indeed!" (Act
III, Scene 5, Lines 118-28)

*Juliet's out-and-out refusal to marry Paris
demonstrates her strength of will that shows how much
she has matured over the course of a few days. Her
language takes on the same shifting, deceptive quality
that we've seen in other characters. Juliet's true
affection requires her to make her words double.*

18. "NURSE
Faith, here it is.
Romeo is banish'd; and all the world to nothing,
That he dares ne'er come back to challenge you;
Or, if he do, it needs must be by stealth.
Then, since the case so stands as now it doth,
I think it best you married with the county.
O, he's a lovely gentleman!
Romeo's a dishclout to him: an eagle, madam,
Hath not so green, so quick, so fair an eye
As Paris hath. Beshrew my very heart,
I think you are happy in this second match,
For it excels your first: or if it did not,

Your first is dead; or 'twere as good he were,
As living here and you no use of him.
JULIET
Speakest thou from thy heart?
Nurse
And from my soul too;
Or else beshrew them both.
JULIET
Amen!" (Act III, Scene 5, Lines 225-41)

Juliet's Nurse has been her closest friend and her surrogate mother all through her life. In encouraging Juliet to give up on Romeo and enter into bigamy with Paris, she demonstrates her own limitations. Her suggestion that Juliet might even prefer Paris to Romeo for his good looks reveals how little she understands Juliet's conviction and sincerity. The suggestion is a real betrayal, and Juliet treats it accordingly.

19. "Give me, give me! O, tell not me of fear!" (Act IV, Scene 2, Line 123)

In moments of extremity, Juliet often speaks briefly instead of delivering a long soliloquy. This urgent plea for Friar Lawrence's drug demonstrates the depth of her desperation—and her courage. Her language here is at once brave and childish.

20. "Farewell! God knows when we shall meet again.
I have a faint cold fear thrills through my veins,
That almost freezes up the heat of life:
I'll call them back again to comfort me:
Nurse! What should she do here?
My dismal scene I needs must act alone.
Come, vial.
What if this mixture do not work at all?

Shall I be married then to-morrow morning?
No, no: this shall forbid it: lie thou there.
What if it be a poison, which the friar
Subtly hath minister'd to have me dead,
Lest in this marriage he should be dishonour'd,
Because he married me before to Romeo?
I fear it is: and yet, methinks, it should not,
For he hath still been tried a holy man.
How if, when I am laid into the tomb,
I wake before the time that Romeo
Come to redeem me? there's a fearful point!
Shall I not, then, be stifled in the vault,
To whose foul mouth no healthsome air breathes
in,
And there die strangled ere my Romeo comes?
Or, if I live, is it not very like,
The horrible conceit of death and night,
Together with the terror of the place,—
As in a vault, an ancient receptacle,
Where, for these many hundred years, the bones
Of all my buried ancestors are packed:
Where bloody Tybalt, yet but green in earth,
Lies festering in his shroud; where, as they say,
At some hours in the night spirits resort;—
Alack, alack, is it not like that I,
So early waking, what with loathsome smells,
And shrieks like mandrakes' torn out of the earth,
That living mortals, hearing them, run mad:—
O, if I wake, shall I not be distraught,
Environed with all these hideous fears?
And madly play with my forefather's joints?
And pluck the mangled Tybalt from his shroud?
And, in this rage, with some great kinsman's
bone,
As with a club, dash out my desperate brains?
O, look! methinks I see my cousin's ghost

Seeking out Romeo, that did spit his body
Upon a rapier's point: stay, Tybalt, stay!
Romeo, Romeo, Romeo! Here's drink. I drink to
thee." (Act IV, Scene 3, Lines 15-60)

*The bravery that Juliet exhibited in the previous
quotation continues here. Juliet, still so young,
considers for a moment calling her mother and the
Nurse back to comfort her, but at last steels herself. She
imagines the potential betrayal of Friar Lawrence—
after all, none of the adults around her has proven very
reliable—and the appalling horrors of the tomb. This
queasy, fleshly imagery demonstrates what Juliet is
facing and gives us a foretaste of the Capulet tomb
we'll soon be visiting. Juliet's morbid fascination with
the reality of death here helps to prepare the audience
for the play's tragic end.*

21. "If I may trust the flattering truth of sleep,
My dreams presage some joyful news at hand:
My bosom's lord sits lightly in his throne;
And all this day an unaccustom'd spirit
Lifts me above the ground with cheerful
thoughts.
I dreamt my lady came and found me dead—
Strange dream, that gives a dead man leave to
think!—
And breathed such life with kisses in my lips,
That I revived, and was an emperor.
Ah me! how sweet is love itself possess'd,
When but love's shadows are so rich in joy!"
(Act V, Scene 1, Lines 1-12)

*Romeo's second dream prefigures a reunion with Juliet
and a resurrection through her. This is another moment
of painful dramatic irony: We know that this reunion*

won't happen. However, that Juliet's kiss revives the dead Romeo in this dream suggests a tiny grace note of hope: Romeo's earlier dream of death and doom is certainly coming true, so perhaps the two will reunite after death. Dreams, here as elsewhere, have a complicated relationship to reality: The truth they contain isn't necessarily legible to the dreamer.

22. "ROMEO
Come hither, man. I see that thou art poor:
Hold, there is forty ducats: let me have
A dram of poison, such soon-speeding gear
As will disperse itself through all the veins
That the life-weary taker may fall dead
And that the trunk may be discharged of breath
As violently as hasty powder fired
Doth hurry from the fatal cannon's womb.
Apothecary
Such mortal drugs I have; but Mantua's law
Is death to any he that utters them.
ROMEO
Art thou so bare and full of wretchedness,
And fear'st to die? famine is in thy cheeks,
Need and oppression starveth in thine eyes,
Contempt and beggary hangs upon thy back;
The world is not thy friend nor the world's law;
The world affords no law to make thee rich;
Then be not poor, but break it, and take this.
Apothecary
My poverty, but not my will, consents.
ROMEO
I pay thy poverty, and not thy will." (Act V,
Scene 1, Lines 62-80)

The play spends a surprising amount of time on this haunted, starved, and weather-beaten apothecary—a

23. "How oft when men are at the point of death
Have they been merry! which their keepers call
A lightning before death: O, how may I
Call this a lightning? O my love! my wife!
Death, that hath suck'd the honey of thy breath,
Hath had no power yet upon thy beauty:
Thou art not conquer'd; beauty's ensign yet
Is crimson in thy lips and in thy cheeks,
And death's pale flag is not advanced there.
Tybalt, liest thou there in thy bloody sheet?
O, what more favour can I do to thee,
Than with that hand that cut thy youth in twain
To sunder his that was thine enemy?
Forgive me, cousin! Ah, dear Juliet,
Why art thou yet so fair? shall I believe
That unsubstantial death is amorous,
And that the lean abhorred monster keeps
Thee here in dark to be his paramour?
For fear of that, I still will stay with thee;
And never from this palace of dim night
Depart again: here, here will I remain
With worms that are thy chamber-maids; O, here
Will I set up my everlasting rest,
And shake the yoke of inauspicious stars
From this world-wearied flesh. Eyes, look your
last!
Arms, take your last embrace! and, lips, O you
The doors of breath, seal with a righteous kiss
A dateless bargain to engrossing death!
Come, bitter conduct, come, unsavoury guide!
Thou desperate pilot, now at once run on

The dashing rocks thy sea-sick weary bark!
Here's to my love! O true apothecary,
Thy drugs are quick. Thus with a kiss I die." (Act
V, Scene 3, Lines 88-120)

Romeo's last speech, agonizingly drawn out, is constructed to inflict maximal suffering on the audience. As Romeo notices that Juliet doesn't look dead at all, there's still the hope that Juliet might wake up before Romeo can kill himself. She doesn't, and Romeo's last words bring many of the play's familiar themes (fate in the stars, the linkage between love and mortality) to their culmination.

24. "Yea, noise? then I'll be brief. O happy dagger!
This is thy sheath. There rust, and let me die."
(Act V, Scene 3, Lines 174-75)

Juliet's last words, conversely, are brief and (literally) to the point. She has no time to reflect on mortality or beauty: Her love drives her to quick and final action. There's a degree of role-reversal in the lovers' last minutes. Juliet's use of Romeo's knife as the instrument of her self-destruction suggests a kind of courage that, to a Renaissance audience, might have a masculine flavor. Moreover, for the first time in the play, a sexual double-entendre has a depressing and tragic cadence rather than a playful one.

25. "A glooming peace this morning with it brings;
The sun, for sorrow, will not show his head:
Go hence, to have more talk of these sad things;
Some shall be pardon'd, and some punished:
For never was a story of more woe
Than this of Juliet and her Romeo." (Act V,
Scene 3, Lines 316-21)

The Prince gets the play's last word, and serves as a counterpart to the Chorus. He sums up its tragic events in the language of storytelling. There's the sense that the final reconciliation of the Montagues and Capulets has a legendary quality—as indeed, now, it does.

1. How do Romeo and Juliet uphold and subvert other characters' ideas about what it is to be a man or a woman—especially around sexuality?

2. Why might the death of Mercutio, who might at first seem like a figure of pure comic relief, be such an important turning point in the play?

3. *Romeo and Juliet* features a cavalcade of punny jokes. Why might the play use the wordplay it does? How does wordplay relate to the play's themes?

4. Choose one of the play's major recurring images, like the moon, stars, and sun; light and darkness; plants and flowers; birds. Then trace the appearance of your chosen motif throughout the play. How does Shakespeare's use of the image change as the play goes on?

5. The Nurse is full of goofy humor, but her attempt to persuade Juliet to marry Paris is deadly serious. Why is the Nurse's failure to understand Juliet's love for Romeo so devastating to Juliet? How is the Nurse meaningful beyond her role as a clown?

6. Consider why the famous balcony scene is structured the way it is. How does it shape the viewer's emotional understanding of the play? Why might it be set on a balcony, and in a garden? How does the imagery of this scene relate to some of the play's themes?

7. Consider Friar Lawrence's speech on the properties of herbs. How do his ideas about moderation play out in

his own behavior—and how does the play seem to support or undermine those ideas?

8. *Romeo and Juliet* is one of Shakespeare's most beloved plays, and one of the most frequently adapted. Pick a scene, and compare at least two film versions of it. How do different directors visually communicate the play's ideas and themes? How might you present the play if you were directing it?

9. Compare one of Romeo's monologues to one of Juliet's (for instance, you might compare Romeo's speech in the garden to Juliet's "Gallop apace, you fiery-footed steeds" speech. How do their language, style, and imagery relate to each other, and how do they differ? What can you learn about the two lovers from the way they speak?

10. Many of the play's characters seem skeptical or cynical about love. How does the play explore the complexities of love—its power, its silliness, its beauty, its dangers?

Made in United States
North Haven, CT
19 May 2022

19322115R00036